NIGHTMARE ON PENNSYLVANIA AVENUE

WALTER RANDALL BANNISTER

THIS BOOK IS DEDICATED TO

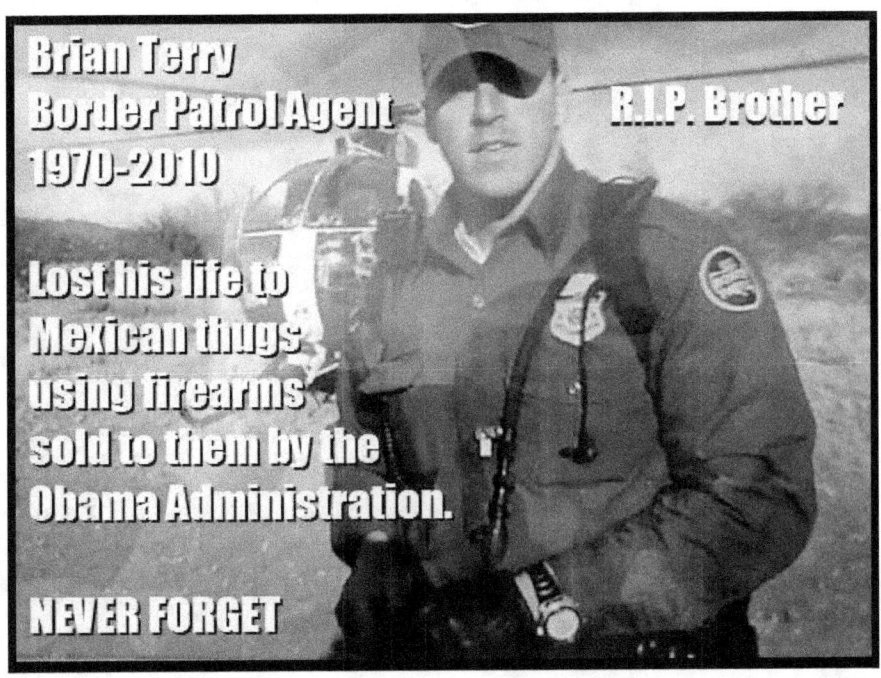

Brian Terry
Border Patrol Agent   R.I.P. Brother
1970-2010

Lost his life to
Mexican thugs
using firearms
sold to them by the
Obama Administration.

NEVER FORGET

CONTENTS

MY OWN POLITICAL VIEW

Stop undeclared wars which are daily costing American lives and billions of tax dollars; Stop reckless spending, including foreign aid, and take care of America's domestic needs; End debt financing of both Federal and State governments; Terminate the Federal income tax, and restore a tariff based revenue system; Immediately end international trade agreements such as NAFTA, WTO, and the proposed FTAA Totally and Completely Secure Our Nations Borders Defend America's moral values; keep God in the pledge of allegiance and on our nation's coinage. Fully protect the right to life of the innocent unborn; Support high standards in education, including school vouchers, private schools and home schooling; Encourage revitalized domestic oil production and nuclear power generation. Defend Second Amendment rights; Restore a Constitutional, asset based, money system;

1

"Obama Wins!"
November 9th, 2008
1 Peter 2:13-17; Romans 13:1-7

Obama wins! The newspaper shouts out at me Wednesday morning. The news commentators are virtually dancing in glee on TV. The gays in San Francisco are literally dancing in the street. The TV shows the terrorist and our enemies overseas dancing in the street. Their man won! Liberals have won at almost every level. Teens can continue to go get an abortion without their parent's knowledge or consent.

Only a few conservative values pass. Same sex marriage is defeated – but only narrowly. Hollywood won. The left wing media won. Socialism won. The liberals have a majority in the house and senate. They have the presidency and the United States Supreme Court. I fear our country is in a downward spiral that will quickly result in our destruction as the nation we once knew.

Our forefathers wisely created a government that had a balance of power between the legislative, judicial and the executive powers - and now that balance has shifted away from everything our country was founded on. Now that one party is in power – we may see the change they wanted. The killing of millions of babies probably will continue.

Homosexuals and perverts will continue to devour our children as they actively promote their agenda in our public schools. Not only will they educate them in detestable homosexual practices – but they may actively enlist them in their life style. Christians and people of value may continue

to diminish and could very like soon become the enemy of the state. As I said last week, we will be called haters and exclusionary because of our belief in the Bible.

But we knew this was going to happen, didn't we? Those of us who believe we are living in the end times saw this coming. Paul wrote 2000 years ago:

But mark this: there will be terrible times in the last days. People will be lovers of themselves, lovers of money, boastful, proud, abusive, disobedient to their parents, ungrateful, unholy, without love, unforgiving, slanderous, without self-control, brutal, not lovers of the good, treacherous, rash, conceited, lovers of pleasure rather than lovers of God, having a form of godliness but denying its power. Have nothing to do with them." 2 Timothy 3:1-5

Paul sums it up in verse 12. He says: In fact, everyone who wants to live a godly life in Christ Jesus will be persecuted, while evil men and imposters will go from bad to worse, deceiving and being deceived."

That doesn't paint a very bright picture for the Christian, does it? But I have good news for you. God is still on the throne! God is still in control. When the dust has settled and the air is clear – we will emerge victorious with Him. And one day every knee will bow and every tongue will confess that Jesus is Lord.

So what are we to do now? How should the Christian react to all this? Well, a lot of Christian were deceived and voted for this change. This couldn't have happened without the Christian vote. Some voted for Obama simply because he is black – and that is as racists as the one who didn't vote for him because he is black. Some Christians, with their vote, unwittingly promoted the anti-Christian agenda. The blood of countless infants will be on their hands. The homosexual perversion will be their doing. The anti-home and anti-Christian agenda will be partly their fault. And many good Christian people will be responsible for what is to come in the days ahead.

Aren't you glad God is forgiving and merciful? He still loves us. He still is for us in spite of unwise choices we make – but we will live with the consequences of those choices. And the bible gives us some clear direction on what to do and how to live. We've been in this place before. Christians have always gone against the mainstream. We've always been the minority – and always will in this life. Christians have been martyred since the first century. Christians have been persecuted since the time of Christ. We have some experience with this. Let's take a look at what the bible says we should do.

"Submit yourselves for the Lord Sake to every authority instituted among men: whether to the king, as the supreme authority, or to governors, who are sent to punish those who do wrong and to commend those who do right."

That verse is a little confusing to a lot a people. Is it saying that we are to blindly go along with anyone in power? Are we to submit to the authorities – no matter what? Or are those who do right and punish wrong the only ones that have God's authority – and we are to submit only to them? The others do not have the authority to make you disobey

5

God.

I don't think Christians are to submit to evil. We aren't to blindly accept what is contrary to the Bible. Right is still right and wrong is still wrong. And it isn't defined by popular opinion. It is defined by God in His Word. But the first instruction, after having said all that, is to have a submissive spirit. We need to just do good – and be good. It doesn't matter what anyone else is doing. The Word of God says, "For is it God's will that by doing good you should silence the ignorant talk of foolish men." 1 Peter 2:15

Now, anytime the bible uses the word foolish or fool – it means 'godless'. Psalm 14:1 says, "The fool says in his heart, 'there is no God'". So the way we are to silence those people who have no room for God in their hearts, is by doing good. I don't know what that means for you. For me it means to do God's will in my life no matter what. Goodness is a fruit of the Spirit. The Bible says that Jesus went around doing good. We need to do the same. Do the best you can to do good works – not to earn your salvation - Jesus already did that. But that is what a Christian is to do. That's the expression of Jesus living in your heart. Jesus can still go around doing good – through you. So do good. Be loving. Be kind. Be gentle. Be Christlike in all you do.

Secondly, we are to show proper respect to everyone. (v.17). We don't have to agree with them. We don't have to even like them. But every person you meet is someone Jesus loves so much – that He died for them. Treat every creation of God's with respect. The one who respects others reflects God's character. Have you ever seen anyone who used 'sir' and 'madam' and opened doors for ladies? He didn't do it because the one he was honoring deserved it. He did it because HE was the kind of man he was. Respect starts on the inside. It has little to do with those we are respecting. We need to always be respectful.

Thirdly, love the brotherhood of believers (v. 17). Care about God's people. Sacrifice for them. Give yourself and your will up for them. That is the expression of love. Hebrews 10:25 says, "Let us not give up meeting together, as some are in the habit of doing, but let us encourage one another – and all the more as you see the Day approaching."

We need the encouragement of each other. We need to study and discuss God's Word and its eternal truths and how it applies to our every day lives. We need to sharpen our skills and work together to become better at accomplishing the mission our Lord gave us. We just need to become better at loving one another. "Love covers a multitude of faults." Love the believers.

Then we are to "Fear God", fourthly. That means we are to respect Him, love Him, and serve Him. Those that fear God believe in a judgment day. They believe He is a reward of those who seek Him and do His will. They believe that those who remain unrepentant will come to judgment and be condemned. Those who fear God live their lives realizing that they must be accountable to God for their actions and they desire to hear His blessed words, "Well done, good and faithful servant. Enter into the joy of your Lord." Fear God, in spite of all – even if those who do not fear God come into power and control. Don't fear them. Fear God. He is the one who matters. He is the One we will be standing before one day. He is the One who we must give an accounting of our actions to.

Finally, we are to honor the king. That's kind of hard if your beliefs are different that his. A lot of pastors, at pastor's and wives retreat, this last week were pretty upset with the election. But we are to respect and honor the position. We don't have to agree with it. That speaks more of who we are that who they are. God wants us to be gracious and kind. He wants us to be respectful and polite. There were a lot of people I talked to those who hated – absolutely hated - the last president. They disrespected him and dishonored this honorable and godly man. They lied about him and blamed him for things that he had no control over. Let's us not be like that. Let's honor the king. Barack Obama is NOT our king. He is our president. We need to honor him and support him. We need to pray for Him. He has testified to being a Christian. He has used Jesus' name as Lord. If that is true, we need to so surround him with prayer that no matter what far left counsel he is getting – he will listen to the Lord and be led of the Holy Spirit. God can use him to bring the right kind of change to our country. Wouldn't it be something if he appointed godly judges to the Supreme Court? Would it be something if God used him to strike down the killing of America's babies? Wouldn't it be something if God used Him to bring America back to God? Is anything too difficult for God? We need to pray for our leaders more than ever before.

There are some people who hate our president just because he is black and would assassinate him if they could. We need to pray for his protection. We need to pray God would get a hold of his heart. We need to pray that God would break his will and shape his spirit.

Don't allow the enemy to make you bitter and angry and ungodly. Above all – especially in times of difficulty – live a Christ like life. Let love and mercy and kindness overflow in you.

Don't ever let anything DEChristianize you!
In my devotional reading, I just finished the book of Revelation. I've read the end of the story. I know how it will all turn out. And we will be persecuted and even killed at some time or another. But in the end – we will win. When the dust has settled and the air is cleared – we will emerge triumphantly with our King. So don't lose hope. Don't be discouraged. God is still on the throne. And now – more than ever – we need to be the Christlike witnesses the world needs to see.

"The Battle Belongs to the Lord"

2
OBAMANATION

Jeremiah 1:16-19 2:7-19

Jeremiah the weeping prophet was charged by God to deliver his message to the people of Israel and like us, they had forsaken the Lord and had followed after other gods. Gods of gold, silver and stone gods that could not save them.

Proverbs 29:2 (King James Version)
When the righteous are in authority, the people rejoice: but when the wicked beareth rule, the people mourn.

We have cause to morn in America the land of the not so free anymore!!!

• Reverse the pro-life Mexico City Policy -
Accomplished by Executive Order on January 23, 2009.
• Restore funding to the UNFPA –
• Increase Title X Funding (Planned Parenthood Funding Stream) to $700M - Title X Domestic Family Planning received an increase of about $7.5 million for a total of $307M. (2.5% increase) More requested for FY 2010.
• Rescind Conscience Protections for Medical Providers – person in the medical field will be forced to participate in abortion or lose there license.

• Strike Abortion Budgetary Restrictions Kemp-Kasten language limiting funds for organizations connected to coercive abortion practices weakened in FY 2009 budget.
• Provide $1B for International Family Planning -

International Family Planning received an increase of $88 million for a total of $545 million. (19% percent increase over $457 million in FY08).

• Select Pro-Abortion Judicial Nominees David Hamilton nominated for U.S. 7th Circuit Court of Appeals.
• Choose Pro-Abortion Federal Appointees Achieved with nominations of Kathleen Sebelius, Janet Napolitano, David Ogden, Elena Kagan, Ellen Moran, Dawn Johnsen, and more.
• Review Policies that Restrict Access to Emergency Contraception FDA approved access to Plan B for 17 year olds.
• Reduce the Cost of Birth Control at College Health Centers Nominal drug pricing for university and community clinics included in FY 2009 Budget.
1) A letter was sent out to all law enforcement agencies that stated: "Persons who criticize the government, are pro-life, support the right to bear arms and person who are right wing conservatives are to be considered a terrorist threat."
2) Two black pastors were arrested in Washington DC for praying on a public sidewalk. Even
Sprinklers were turned on to wet them down first.
3) Hate crimes bill (pedophile protection bill) expected to pass, this will make It illegal to
Preach Against homosexuality.
4) 3.5 Trillion dollar budget. (Break our nation)
5) Anti Gun legislation proposed.
6) Negative stance toward Israel.
7) Meeting with our enemies: leading Hamas official endorsed Barack Obama stating, "I do believe [Obama] is like John Kennedy, a great man with a great principle"

8) Refused to pray publicly at the national day of prayer.

I hope you can see where all of this is headed.

First: You take away free speech with Hate crimes bill then with a Hate propaganda bill /hate speech legislation to silence the opposition.

Second: Remove free press with reinstating the fairness doctrine and start fining all news and information outlets that appose your point of view.

Third: Remove parental rights, take the children from parents and indoctrinate them with new global socialistic training at government training camps.

Fourth: Remove gun ownership for private citizens so they cannot appose you by force.

Fifth: Remove a person's right to object to performing adorations, mercy killings and forced sterilizations based on conscience.

Sixth: Orchestrate or allow a large terrorist attack as an excuse to in act marshal law and suspend future elections due to on going war.

You see know Jesus Christ Know freedom. NO Jesus No freedom.

Jer 2:7-8 God gave us this fertile land but we have defiled it with homosexuality and the blood of the innocent. Our spiritual leaders are not standing up in unison. We are now worshiping the gods of gold (money) wood (fancy houses) Stone (mother earth)

Our new priest are secular scientists that promise eternal life if they can just create enough babies and kill them for there body parts so you can live forever!

Jer 2:12 be appalled at this! Shudder with great horror! God declares!

Look at Jer 2:13- Two sins America has committed two sins forsaken the life giving spring of Jesus Christ and dug mud hole that can't hold water.

We as a nation are dieing of spiritual thirst!

We have become our own enemy Jer 2:19 Your wickedness will punish you! Your backsliding will rebuke you. It is evil and bitter when we forsake the Lord our God!

Vs 20 (read) I the sixties we declared
free love-
freedom from the 10 commandments
freedom from restraint.
And now with this administration freedom from
Christianity-Christ-prayer-Bible-God

God has called us to stand for righteousness not just to sit and pray.

It's like we are leaning on a shovel and praying for a hole. Faith without works is dead and many silent Christians today have a dead faith.

Or they say well God said it will happen so let us just sit

idly by while our country latterly goes to Hell!

If You Do Not Stand Against Evil, You Stand For It. (silent affirmation)

James 2:17 Even so faith, if it has no works, is dead Eph 6:13 Wherefore take unto you the whole armour of God, that ye may be able to withstand in the evil day, and having done all, to stand.

Listen to this verse having done all to stand!!
1. Have we done all there is to stand?
2. Have we even made a stand?
3. Have we stood for righteousness or nothing?

We must speak out against evil.

Now I'm sure some of you are setting there saying judge not lest ye be judged. I have even had so called Christians quote me this verse as an excuse not to do or say anything about the evil going on in our nation.

Truth: Our leaders in congress our president our judges have not judged correctly they have called what is evil good and what is good evil. The majority of our leaders are now a bunch of God hating, homosexual promoting, gun grabbing, baby killing, Christian imprisoning, and freedom stealing, communist, socialistic, bigoted haters of righteousness.

"There are six things the Lord HATES, seven that are detestable to him: haughty eyes, a lying tongue, hands that shed innocent blood, a heart that devises wicked schemes, feet that are quick to rush into evil, a false witness who pours out lies and a man who stirs up dissension among brothers" (Proverbs 6:16-19).

And if we acknowledge the Holy God as our Father, perhaps, there is also a tendency for us to echo what David said:

"Do I not HATE those who hate you, O Lord, and abhor those who rise up against you? I have nothing but hatred for them; I count them my enemies" (Ps. 139:22). Also his words in Psalm 119:104, "I gain understanding from your precepts; therefore I HATE every wrong path" (also verse 128).

I know the Bible says that we are to submit to the governing authorities we the people are still the governing authority in this nation last time I checked.

Another point: last time I checked God was is control and we are to submit to Him and He is calling us to make a stand by prayer and physically do something to bring him honor!!!

You can start by giving your life to Jesus Christ and then Giving your life to the cause of Jesus Christ and go into the entire world (including government) and preach the gospel to all nations! Especially The United States of America!

3
BRINGING AMERICA BACK TO GOD

JUDGES CHAPTERS 1 & 2

This book (the book of Judges) records the history of the nation of Israel for 305 years after the death of Joshua. Israel declined, backslid, and got away from God. And in this new study we will see many frightening parallels between Israel and America.

Israel was established by God Himself, and God gave Himself to them. He also gave them the law--the 10 commandments and the covenant. And He gave them Canaan, the best land of the earth at that time. And so God gave them the Lord, the law, and the land.

God only asked them for one thing in return--that they would love Him, obey Him, and serve Him. What did Israel do? They denied the Lord, they defied the law, and they defiled the land. So, God had to judge them.

The parallel with America is obvious and alarming. No nation has ever had a Christian beginning like the USA. We too have been given the Lord, the law, and a land, and we've denied Him, defied Him, and our land is being defiled.

1. America has denied the Lord.

The Lord is slowly but steadily being expelled from every public venue. It started in the public schools, and has spread to public places, court houses, our coins, our pledge of allegiance, and on and on to the point where today we are fighting battles about what we can even say in the church! It is no longer just about the separation of church and state but rather the separation of America from the God Who founded her and has so blessed her!

This last week a high school football team and its cheerleaders came under fire. The players and cheerleaders were all in agreement. They all wanted the team to enter the field, bursting thru a large paper banner with an inspirational Bible verse on it. It wasn't school sanctioned, and no one involved had any problem with it ... but guess who did have a problem? The ACLU! "The American Communist...ummm...Civil Liberties Union". You could call them the Anti Christian Liberals Union. Actually, I don't know why they aren't called the UUUU, for they are Unamerican, uncivil, and unlibertarian!

The ACLU has been used by Satan as a tool for many years, tearing apart the God woven fabric of our society.

America has denied the Lord...

2. America has defied the law.
The Supreme Court says that it is against the law to display the 10 Commandments in a public place, [though their building displays them!] reasoning that if you display them people might ponder them and if so, they might obey them, and that would be a violation of the separation of church and state. We are doing just what Israel did. It is now the official position of our government that the 10 commandments are dangerous! Wouldn't want kids in school to see 'thou shalt not kill' because what if they obeyed it!

ladies, what if you broke down in the worst part of town and had to walk, after dark, to find help. While you walk a group of

4 men leave a house you are passing and begin walking just behind you. How do you feel? As you listen to what they are saying you notice they are talking about God, and have just left a Bible study session. You turn around and see they are all carrying Bibles. How do you feel now?

The new direction our once Christian nation is now going in is just foolish, and contrary to basic common sense. We don't force our beliefs on anyone, but we have allowed the world to chip away at our core of morality.

Like Israel, we have denied the Lord, defied the law...

3. America has defiled the land.
We've done this in many ways, but perhaps the #1 way is found in the spilled blood of aborted babies.

God took away His glory from His people Israel when they did such things. And I believe He is in the process of removing Himself from the good old US of A. We need a national revival. We need a moral and spiritual awakening. I don't know what it's gonna take. If 9/11 wasn't enough, what will be enough?

The book of Judges is the record of God raising up 13 men to deliver Israel from backsliding in order to bring about national revival.

Our outline is best understood by an illustration of 'the family fortune.' When a family becomes rich there are 3 stages which seem to always occur:
• The first generation generates the fortune.
• The second generation speculates their fortune, thru a series

of compromises and foolish decisions.

• The third generation dissipates the fortune and it is gone.

That is exactly how it works with a nation. There is a
generation that generates the freedom, then a generation that
speculates it away, and finally, a generation that dissipates it
until completely gone, and freedom is no more. If you don't
believe this, you need to study those nations that have forgotten
God in history.

Generation - speculation - dissipation

A. Generation

What do we know about the generation of Israel that entered
into the Promised Land? Under General Joshua Israel was
given by God victory after victory. Walls came tumbling down,
and kings were subdued. They won victories they never could
have apart from the power of God.

And that's just how it is with America. Go back to our first
war, the Revolutionary War. Britain had more men, more
money, better machinery...it was a truly a David and Goliath
scenario but God was on our side and we won!

Patrick Henry gave the speech which sparked the revolution in
1775. He said, "Is life so dear, or peace so sweet, as to be
purchased at the price of chains or slavery? Forbid it, Almighty
God! I know not what course others may take but as for me;
give me liberty or give me death!"

It was 'game on.' And we won that war, and George
Washington became our first president. When he took office he
placed his hand on the Holy Bible. He finished taking the oath
and kissed the Bible. His first official act was to lead the entire
congress in a 2 hour worship session. I wonder what the ACLU

would have said about that.

In one of his inaugural addresses he said, "No people can be bound to acknowledge and adore the invisible hand which conducts the affairs of men more than the people of the United States. Every step by which they have advanced to the character of an independent nation seems to have been distinguished by some token of providential agency." In plain English he said, it is God Who got us this far, and we had better not forget it!

Our founding fathers made it abundantly clear that this land was founded on God and the Bible. The Bible was the first and only book to be used in public schools for years.

Generation...

B. Speculation
Succeeding generations in Israel began to squander it all away. 2:1-2 God says, look at all I have done for you. I delivered you from slavery, fed you with manna, guided you and guarded you into the Promised Land. Now look at you...why have you done this?!

v. 7 The Joshua generation saw first hand the great works of God.
v. 10 What a sad verse! This means that the Joshua generation failed to pass their values on to their children. This has happened in America since 1960, and look where we are at today. Americans today are brainwashed by humanism, situational ethics, and relativism. We do not understand our moral foundations and the spiritual principles upon which this nation was founded. We are trying to rewrite history and remove God from our land.

The saddest verse in this book is the last one...

Judges 21:25 In those days there was no king in Israel: every man did that which was right in his own eyes.
They became a people with no absolutes...no standard to live by. Is that not the nation you and I live in today? Aren't these parallels frightening?

Barna Research shows that 67% of Americans say there is no such thing as absolute truth. They say that right and wrong are not clear...what is wrong for you is not necessarily wrong for me. If that doesn't scare you, consider that they did the same survey in evangelical churches like this one and among Sunday morning attendees 52% said the same thing! Imagine, Christians saying there's no black and white, right and wrong!

Look how Israel got to this point. It was thru a series of compromises.

2:2a God had told them to drive the enemy out of the land, and further, not to have anything to do with them. They were to separate themselves from the world, just as we are supposed to do today.

1. The Canaanites that they feared.
1:19 They were afraid. They could have trusted in God and won, but they were afraid to try with those who were strong. They said, these people are impenetrable. We cannot conquer them. Therefore we might as well learn to accommodate them, surrender to them, and learn to live with them.

And there are some Canaanites that we are fearing in America today:

• Many of our leaders want to surrender in the war on terror. They say we are losing and we might as well quit trying to win. We need to sit down and negotiate with the terrorists, and stop trying to police the world. And in so doing we invite them to come to us.

• Many politicians today are calling for an end to the war on drugs. They say that we have lost, so we should surrender and legalize it. Because if we legalize it we can control it, they say. Yeah, just like we have full control over alcohol, right? Former Clinton Surgeon General Jocelyn Elders is a major proponent of this thinking. But trying to control drugs by legalizing them is like trying to control a fire with gasoline.

• Many parents are surrendering in the area of sexual promiscuity. They throw up their hands and say, well, you're not gonna be good, so just be careful. Here, wear protection. Now what message does that send to a young person? ill.--We are putting ambulances at the bottom of the cliff when we are supposed to be putting fences at the edge of the cliff!

It's time we get back to confronting our culture with the truth of God and His Word. Young people, God wants you to be pure and chaste. He wants you to be a virgin when you get married, not passed around like a bottle of Gatorade in a football huddle!

We've become afraid of the confrontation, and way too sensitive about how we might offend someone who has gone too far. Well, whom shall I offend? Man, or God? The truth is offensive, but it is our only hope.

John 8:32 And ye shall know the truth, and the truth shall make you free.

• We've become so politically correct about homosexuality that it has become wrong to say anything about it. We say we personally are against it, but leave it as a personal decision and ok in our society in spite of what God says and in spite of what always happens to a society when they go that route. And we give them more than just equal status, but exalted status! [special status-and that makes the rest of us be discriminated status!]

• And now, something new, and never before considered in America. Socialism. Ignoring the plight of other countries who have tried it, we are beginning to slide down a dead end, one way, no U-turn street that leads from Capitalism upon which we were founded to socialism, communism, and becoming a nation with no wealth, no freedom, and no real reason to work for anything!

We are at the tail end of the speculation generation, and it's getting scary!

The Canaanites that they feared...

2. The Canaanites that they favored.
1:28 They said, look, we can use these people. They made slaves of them, in spite of the fact that God said not to have anything to do with them. Sure they are wicked, but there's some good can that come out of them.

What about America today? Legalized gambling, the lottery, and such things. Look at the gain we can find from something that many consider only to be bad. Why, we'll build roads and schools, and generate lots of tax dollars! Isn't it sad that our government has turned itself into a pimp? Think about it. A pimp puts women on street corners to lure in men, in order that he, the pimp, might profit from their vice. And our government now encourages its citizens to participate in a vice so they can profit. They say, look at the revenue we can generate!

It's time we stop saying look at what we can gain and start asking, what might we lose by doing this?!

Now we're turning to borrowing, and borrowing not just from banks, but from the world, especially China, who now owns us. What's more, we're borrowing from our children and future generations who will never be able to pay it back...but hey, that's their problem!

If you disagree with me on this, that's fine, but when you do, you are further illustrating just how far we have come

from our founding generation!

Just like Israel, we are favoring the world. For the first time ever we have a president of the world, who apologizes for us, and is one of them. He's a world citizen much more than an American. But once he works his miracles on us maybe he'll finally be able to be proud to be one of us!

Canaanites that they feared, favored...

3. The Canaanites that they fellowshipped with.
1:32 Hey, these people aren't that bad. They may worship different gods but they are good neighbors. We read on and find that Israel learned their wicked ways and entered into their idolatry, including the abortion like sacrificing of their children to Molech.

The cry of our day is, There's nothing wrong with being gay. What they do is their business. I don't see why they couldn't be married or adopting children. And they should have rights of their own, after all, they most often make good neighbors...why can't we all just get along?! I'll tell you why we can't get along, God says they are an abomination and will be our downfall as a society. If we tolerate it we are begging for His judgment. He's done it before, and He'll do it again! [Sodom]

God loves homosexuals and so should we. So we love them, not by accepting their sin, but by confronting it with the truth, the antidote which is their only hope and ours as well!

Israel ended up in the last verse of the book where every man did what was right in his own eyes...and God had to judge. The parallels today are paralyzing when I consider them.

Generation - speculation...

C. Dissipation
2:3 Thorns and snares. Can anyone say, "Illegal immigration?"
2:4 They wept because God was saying, I now lift my hand of protection off of you.

on 9/11 terrorists turned planes into missiles. The next day the late Dr. Jerry Falwell said, "We'd better realize that God is removing His protective hand from this nation." And then he specifically cited our national sins of abortion and homosexuality. The liberal press absolutely crucified him. I've rarely seen such a vicious attack as he endured. But I believe he was right. And God is now using our current administration to give us what we have been asking for. It's change, and we are finding out it is not change we can believe in.

Thorns and snares.

Do you realize that Revelation describes the downfall of a world power like America? It's an economic disaster. Might that be us?

Some say arrogantly, "Would a loving God allow that?" If we ask for it! "Where was God when those students gunned down their classmates at Columbine?" I'll tell you where He was, you expelled him in 1962! You threw out the Bible and prayer and said, God, you're not welcome!

And now we're in a new generation. Could this be the final generation in America? Our forefathers generated so much, our parents speculated it away. Are we the generation that will dissipate it until it is completely gone? We are one generation away from losing our country. This new series will continue thru Judges looking at the judgment we have been asking for.

Is there any hope? Where there's God, there's still hope! 2:16 God would always rather forgive than to judge...but if we insist, well, we should be afraid.

ill.--a benevolent gentleman during the civil war saw a young lady being auctioned off as a slave. He began to bid just above every bid he heard until he finally won the auction, paying a very high price. They say that after winning he began to walk away, and she followed him. He said, "Young lady, I bought you not to own you, but to set you free." "Free?" she asked. "Yes, free to go wherever you want and do what you wish." She replied, "Then I choose to go with you."

After all God has done for America, how can we spit in His face as we are? We need to pray for national revival!

If you are not saved, consider all God has done for you...the high price His Son Jesus paid for you. Will you now choose to be His servant and go with Him?

4

The Wild Man
Genesis 16:11-12

The "Wild Man" is loose on the earth and fulfilling Bible prophecy daily. He has always been here, but today he is ACTIVE. We can call him Ishmael; we can identify him, his descendants, ideologically and spiritually. He is no longer frozen in the Middle East, but has spread, even to a new friend in the White House. At one time the USA was a friend to Israel. The shadow of the wild man has arrived on our scene, within our coasts, but once the wild man's influence permeated our government that friendship changed to suspicion and opposition. We MUST remember, God promised a blessing or cursing based upon how any country or individual treated Israel!

The WILDMAN has constantly tried to gain a foothold of credibility and presence in our country. He was slowly making progress until 9/11, but once his agenda became clear our government and people quickly sought to close off his easy access. This was the 9/12 mentality. Times change however; in the last year his avarice has increased, his cunning doubled and his cause advanced; in the last year he has made progress into the heart of our country and the life of its citizens, and now we find ourselves back in the 9/10 mentality, and worse.

Since 9/11 we have learned a new vocabulary:
We have learned Islam, Mohammad, Allah, Jihad, Taliban, and al Qaeda.

Previous to 9/11 these were silly words, irrelevant words, words used by missionaries or foreigners with towels on their heads and beards. We didn't know these words nor did we care. That is a luxury that we can no longer afford.

These "wild men" are a faceless enemy; they wear no uniform and they fight dirty. Can I make an observation? They do have faces; faces that we can see and they walk among us! Not only do they walk among us with equality, they have garnered a preferred status! They have more protection than you or I have as Christians! What scares me is that they have infiltrated our healthcare institutions; today we call them our "Doctors" and nurses! These wildmen now surround us in ever increasing numbers as we go to work, play and do our daily business. At this point in time they are non-violent, let us hope they stay that way, but don't be taken in! The warning flags are waving!

As for the so called Radicals; they now have special rights! They enjoy these privileges in our courtrooms! Can you believe that we are so foolish to have given them a stage to act out their hatred and murder; to brag about their foul deeds in public court? And the world laughs at our lack of will and interprets it as weakness! We say, "Sure Khalid Sheikh Mohammed, come in and enjoy our freedoms, our courts and juries after you tried to destroy them down the street!" Can we no longer deport anyone?

These "Wildmen" have taken up residence in Congress [Keith Ellison of Minnesota, took his oath of office on the Koran! By the way, who allowed that? America should decide what you swear upon, not the elected one], and they are in our military, but we had better not profile one! It might be the end of your career! You might be prejudiced or politically incorrect even if you are right!

The polls this week reveal that more Americans call what Nidal Malik Hasan did at Ft. Hood a crime than call it terrorism, despite the overwhelming evidence to the contrary.

It walks like a duck, quacks like a duck...and yet, our Major News outlets have taken cover with the pre-9/10 mentality of saying, "Duck? What duck?"

Political correctness permeates the workplaces, the media, government, and sadly, many churches. And it is going to be the end of us as a nation if we don't wake us and start making changes fast.

It's more important to be correct than politically correct. The Bible indicates that if a nation has been given much light from God and then rejects that light, God will give them a mind that cannot even comprehend what is in its best interest.

Our country is doing things that just don't make sense! However, the Bible does warn us that in the last days things will become confusing and that nations who once were blessed of God will do things that are counterproductive even to the point of facing their own destruction.

And don't think this is about Radical Muslims or Moderates; Hasan was an average Moderate Muslim until he came under pressure, then what was deep inside came gushing out. I wonder, what will happen when the entire country of America is squeezed?

The media in our country and world leaders in the UN have made it clear, it isn't about Islam. Why, don't you know? True Islam is peaceful and harmless, they say.

I find the comments of Salmon Rushdie, a Muslim sentenced to death by Muslim clerics over his 1988 book, "The Satanic Verses" very interesting. Rushdie said after 9/11, "The trouble with this …disclaimer is that it isn't true. If this isn't about Islam, then why the worldwide Muslim demonstrations in support of Osama bin Laden and Al Qaeda?" [as quoted in "Israel My Glory" (March/April 2002) 7]

In commenting on the 2001 terrorist attacks on the USA, Franklin

Graham, the son of Billy Graham, said of Islam, "I don't believe this is a wonderful, peaceful religion. When you read the Koran and you read the verses from the Koran, it instructs the killing of the infidel, or those that are non-Muslim." He went on to say, "It wasn't Methodists flying into those buildings, it wasn't Lutherans, it was an attack on this country by people of the Islamic faith." [as quoted by Andrew Webb. "A More Realistic Assessment of Islam." PCA News.com].

In like fashion Chuck Colson has commented, "The Truth is that bin Laden and his followers did not hijack Islam; they simply took it seriously." They are the conservatives who believe and practice their book. This is scary when you see our nation falling for the politically correct notion that we should embrace people of this faith as long as they are not radical. Bush 43 recognized and celebrated Ramadan for PC purposes, and many who call themselves conservatives have bought the lie that Islam is fundamentally a peaceful religion. It is not.

While the overwhelming majority of Arabs are Muslim, most Muslims are not Arab. Although Islam had its origins in the Middle East, the four largest populations of Muslims are Indonesia, India, Bangladesh, and Pakistan. Islam is the fastest growing religion in the world today (there are between 1.2 and 1.5 billion Muslims in the world, nearly 25% making it the 2nd largest religion after Christianity at about 33%).

v. 10 Geographically, about 1/3rd of the land is Arabic or controlled by Arabs. In America, they're at least 7 million and quickly rising.

There were 11,000 converts to Islam each year in the United States in the early 90s (Newsweek, Oct. 30, 1995) and 90% of them are among the black population.

Islam, like Judaism traces its lineage to the patriarch Abraham. The Arabs, however, trace their lineage to the firstborn son of Abraham by Hagar, Ishmael. The Jews trace their lineage to Isaac, the son of Abraham and Sarah who had been promised by God. The war in the Middle East today can be traced back to this Biblical story of who really is the rightful son of Abraham. The truth about the Middle East is that the Palestinians and surrounding Muslim nations will never make a genuine and lasting peace with Israel. They don't want peace – they never wanted peace – they want Israel, all of it, and its inhabitants and supporters dead. And we're all infidels [unbelievers] to them.

The word Islam, meaning submission, says much about the attitude of the followers of Islam.

And while they are among us, they are not of us. Even if not spoken aloud, they have a strong opinion of us and have little or no loyalty to our nation.

Ill.—USA Today published a survey taken of Arab Muslims living in the U.S. concerning their attitude toward the war in Iraq, terrorism, etc. 82% said they would not be willing to allow their son or daughter to fight for this, their country which they have taken an oath to defend. They should be deported if they answer this way. Over ½ stated they would not support war w/ any Arab nation for any reason. By the way, that survey was taken before the first invasion of Iraq [2/6/91]. Much has changed since then!

Let's be clear: not every Muslim is a terrorist or a terrorism supporter, but almost every terrorist today is a Muslim! And because of what the Koran says, every Muslim is high risk to one day rise up against us.

And the wild men following this belief system are convinced that the moment they blow themselves up, taking 'infidels' with them, they will be transported to a heaven where 72 virgins will satiate their lusts and food and drink will satisfy their every appetite. This is why some of the 9/11 terrorists were frequenting porn shops just before their attacks…they were preparing for their move to 'paradise.' Major Hasan was visiting strip clubs just before his rampage.

True Christianity is spread by love and choice – Islam is spread by sword and force.

It is true that some Muslims, like Christians, are willing to die for their faith. Some unfortunately, are also willing to kill for it. In fact the one sure way of earning salvation as a Muslim is to die as a martyr for the faith. They believe that just as Mohammed was whisked immediately to heaven and given several maidens, so will it be done for those who die for the cause of Islam. Those who attacked the World Trade Center and engaged in other acts of terrorism were acting in full accord with the tenets of Islam and the teachings of the Koran. The West, the United States in particular, is seen as corrupting the entire world and worthy of death. The U. S. policy of befriending Israel is particularly seen as harmful to the Muslim people and their cause. The principle of Jihad, or "holy war" is taught in the Koran as a viable tool for the cause of Islam. Evangelism is not so much by the word as it is with the sword. The followers of Mohammad have been the most violent people in the history of the world, and continue to be so to this day — a fact well attested to in history. Jesus taught that we are to love the sinner.

Mohammed taught that the infidel must be killed if he refuses to convert.

Whether you realize it or not, America is at war. How severe will this war be, how long will it last, how many lives will it cost, what form will it take?…these are questions that no one can answer. But make no mistake about it--we are fighting for our way of life, we are fighting for survival. We are fighting against people who are willing to kill us any way they can. We are not playing on a level playing field, as was proven in the Gulf war, we are not allowed to give out Bibles in their lands, even to our own troops, yet they are allowed to build Mosques in our country. And in NYC, Muslim children are allowed to pray in their custom, while our kids cannot.

Now, what about the theory that President Barack Obama is a Muslim? In short I would say that if he is not, he might as well be.

5

Bring Back the Glory
Judges 17-21

Judges 17:6
 In those days there was no king in Israel, but every man did that
which was right in his own eyes.

Judges 21:25
In those days there was no king in Israel: every man did that which
was right in his own eyes.

These final chapters begin and end with these bookends making it
clear that God's people had moved away from moral absolutes.
There was no absolute truth, no authority...they had lost their moral
compass.

In America, we need a moral, spiritual revival or we are doomed.
This is my fear, and it fits well into Bible prophecy.

Anytime a nation goes down and experiences the judgment of God
is happens in this order: Moral decay in the home, then in the
church, and finally in the government.

"As the home goes, so goes the church, and as the church goes, so
goes the nation."

Here's 3 things it will take to bring back the glory to the USA
before it is too late.

1 Families with a Foundation.
v. 1-6 This is not the prophet Micah. He is a spoiled brat. His
mother saved money and he decided to steal it--1100 shekels of

silver. She didn't know whom the thief was, so she pronounced a curse upon him. He got scared when he heard that and returned it, not out of conviction, but out of fear. Rather than scolding him, she blessed him. She was so glad to get the money back. She said she was dedicating it to the Lord and then she made an idol with it.

Of course, the Bible strictly forbids this sort of idolatry. This is how spiritually blind they had become in their apostasy. Far removed from the true worship of God--thinking this was doing God a favor by making an idol to Him.

v. 5 Micah had shelves full of idols...he was steeped in idolatry. Then he appointed his son to become a priest. He didn't qualify, and it wasn't God's way. It is absolute confusion spiritually, and they think they are actually serving God.

So, in this family we have coveting, stealing, cursing, dishonoring of parents, idolatry, and God knows what else. They are morally bankrupt. But if you would have gone to them and confronted them about all of this they would say, "That's your opinion, but this is the way we want to do it." Every man what was right in his own eyes!

This is where America is today. It's not that we don't have enough religion, we are up to our ears in religion. But we have left the absolute Bible authority and truth, standards, and morality. This lack of Bible conviction infiltrates even many families in good Bible churches.

Parents are losing their kids because we are not the examples we need to be. We want them to obey but they see us going our own way personally. Our inconsistencies will be magnified in our kids, just as Micah's mother's issues were magnified in his life. And what we allow in moderation our kids abuse in excess!

In a small Missouri town, 2 preacher's boys were playing with a little dog they found, it was black w/ a white tail, they wanted to keep him. They loved him. Then they heard about a new family who moved in and how they had lost their dog, which was black w/ a white tail. Their preacher dad didn't want to have to give up the dog so he painted the white tail black, and when the new neighbors asked about whether this could be their dog he lied and said, no, the tail is the wrong color. What could they say? Do you know the son's names? Frank and Jesse James, 2 of the most notorious criminals of all time.

As parents we don't get what we want, we get what we are.

And I share this because bringing back the glory to America has much more to do w/ my house and your house than the White House!

We need families w/ a foundation.

2. We need Preachers with Principles.
v. 7 This was a priest, and he is out of a job.
v. 8-13 He has lots of needs, and crosses paths w/ the ungodly Micah, who says, man, have I got a deal for you! He knew his son was not a real priest, so he tries to get this priest to move in. He feels good about being religious. But religion sends more to hell than sin does!

This priest proves himself to be a hireling, because he agrees and just for the money.

18:4 'hired'?

John 10:11-13
11 I am the good shepherd: the good shepherd giveth his life for the sheep.

12 But he that is an hireling, and not the shepherd, whose own the sheep are not, seeth the wolf coming, and leaveth the sheep, and fleeth: and the wolf catcheth them, and scattereth the sheep.

13 The hireling fleeth, because he is an hireling, and careth not for the sheep.

Know how to tell the difference between a true man of God and a hireling? The hireling is committed only to himself and keeping his salary, not the truths of God's Word.

Am I saying the preacher shouldn't be paid? Perish the thought! The Bible says that those that preach the gospel should live of the gospel, matter of fact, they are worthy of double honor.

But the hireling tells people what they want to hear in order to draw a crowd and not offend anyone. He is not called of God, he simply chose a career.

There is not much wrong w/ the USA that could not be readily fixed w/ more true preachers and fewer hirelings. We need a generation that God will get a hold of to preach the uncompromised Word of God! The very topics that are today politically incorrect to talk about are exactly what we need to be talking about. We need preachers who will say, "It's not an alternate lifestyle, homosexuality is an abomination in the sight of God!" Call me homophobic or hateful if you will, but I stand on the absolute authority of God's Word! Which by the way, supports that fact that God loves those sinners.

Our churches are getting so caught up in contemporary worship styles and fads and self help topics we have left off prophetic preaching of the fiery truths of God's Word! I think sincere America is fed up with coffee shop based churches with their interpretive dance, drama skits, and pop psychology from the pulpit.

Hate speech legislation is on its way big time to the USA. It's already against the law for me to endorse a political candidate, but I can preach moral, Biblical truth and encourage you to seek out where candidates stand on the issues. It is also becoming increasingly dangerous to even express disappointment about any of our leaders, especially if they are named Barack Obama. I might have to push the limits on that one in order to preach the truth in good conscience. And I might have to endure more audits in the future!

Galatians 4:16
Am I therefore become your enemy, because I tell you the truth?

Ecclesiastes 7:5
It is better to hear the rebuke of the wise, than for a man to hear the song of fools.

Americans are flocking to hear the songs of fools that are hirelings, not committed to the Word of God!

My job is not to fill this auditorium...it is to fill this pulpit!

To bring back the glory we need families w/ a foundation and preachers with principles...

3. We need Government with God.
Hold on. Hang with me.
17:6 'no king'

I realize God didn't establish Israel as a democracy but as a theocracy, led by God. And I realize America was not established as a theocracy. But if you study history and not try to revise it, there is no question about it...our republic was founded on Biblical, Christian principles. I have heaped up mountains of evidence on this over this series, and it is irrefutable.

And when we take God and Biblical morality out of our nation, it begins to unravel.

We have lost our foundation. Every man does what is right in his own eyes. Politicians don't mind talking about values until you ask them 'whose values' are these values?

Why do you think the homosexuals say they have the right to get married? Because every man does what is right in his own eyes.

Judges keep striking down laws of common sense in favor of political correctness which protects pedophiles and pornographers and criminals of all ranks. We have lost our moral compass!

I like what I'm seeing, however, in Christian America. I see a mass of believers getting involved in politics, running for office, protesting, and taking their stand.

Don't believe the liberal left that says because we believe in God we should just shut up. It's because we believe in God that we ought to speak up!

There are sparks, and we need to fan the flames. Our homes and our churches can affect our government

6
25 Violations of Law
By President Obama and His Administration

1. Obama Administration uses IRS to target conservative, Christian and pro-Israel organizations, donors, and citizens.
2. In an unprecedented attack on the First Amendment, the Obama Justice Department ordered criminal investigations of FOX News reporters for doing their jobs during the 2012 election year.
3. President Obama, throughout his Presidency, has refused to enforce long-established U.S. immigration laws. For example . . .More than 300,000 captured illegal aliens had been processed and were awaiting deportation. But, incredibly, Obama stopped these deportations and ordered the U.S. border patrol to release many of these illegal aliens in violation of law and without explanation.

Congress rejected Obama's so called DREAM ACT – which would have granted permanent residency to many illegal aliens. So Obama enacted his own version of the DREAM ACT by Executive Order, thus directly defying Congress. According to Obama's Executive Order, illegal aliens can stay in America if they are under the age of 30, have been in America for at least five years, are enrolled in school or have graduated from high school, and have committed no felonies.

4. Obama has refused to build a double-barrier security fence along the U.S.-Mexican border in direct violation of the 2006 Secure Fence Act. This law requires that "at least two layers of reinforced fencing" be built along America's 650-mile border with Mexico. So far, just 40 miles of this fence have been built – most of it during the Bush Administration.
5. Obama's unconstitutional assault on your Second Amendment Right to Keep and Bear Arms.

President Obama issued, in one day, 21 separate Executive Orders that attack and undermine your Second Amendment right to keep and bear arms.

Especially egregious is President Obama's Executive Orders amending the **ObamaCare**law to allow doctors and hospitals to investigate which patients own a gun. This outrageous Executive Order could allow the federal government to track and monitor law-abiding gun owners simply because they sought medical care.

6. Obama's assault on Christians and religious freedom.

Obama's Health and Human Services Department has, on its own (without Congressional approval), issued a mandate that all health insurance plans must include coverage for abortion-inducing drugs. As a result, pro-life employers and taxpayers are now effectively required by law to pay for abortions.

This mandate is an unconstitutional attack on the protections for freedom of religion and freedom of conscience in the First Amendment and the 1993 Religious Freedom Restoration Act. This mandate also directly violates the ObamaCare law enacted by Congress, which prohibits any and all taxpayer funds from being used to pay for abortions.

7. Obama forced ObamaCare on an unwilling public through bribery and lying about its cost.

Obama managed to secure passage of ObamaCare by one vote in the Senate by bribing senators. He bribed Senator Ben Nelson of Nebraska with the notorious "Cornhusker Kickback." He bribed Senator Mary Landrieu with the infamous $300 million "Louisiana Purchase."

In addition, Obama knowingly and blatantly lied to America and to Congress about how much ObamaCare would really cost. The cost of ObamaCare to the American people over the next 10 years will not be less than $1 TRILLION, as Obama promised in his nationally televised speech to the nation. Instead, the real cost of ObamaCare to the Federal Treasury is

$2.4 TRILLION, according to the non-partisan Congressional Budget Office.

But the true cost of ObamaCare is more like $10 TRILLION when you factor in the cost to the states, the cost to individual Americans who are now required to purchase Obama-approved health plans (the "Individual Mandate"), the cost of exploding health insurance premiums, the $716 billion ObamaCare steals from Medicare, and the increased cost to businesses of complying with ObamaCare mandates.

8. Operation Fast & Furious.

"Operation Fast & Furious" was the Obama Administration's gun-running scheme that put thousands of American-made semi-automatic weapons in the hands of Mexican drug cartels and resulted in the death of at least one U.S. Border Patrol Agent, Brian Terry. Obama's Attorney General Eric Holder lied to Congress and the public, claiming he didn't know about his Justice Department's **Fast & Furious** operation.

Congress has now held Holder in contempt for defying congressional subpoenas and refusing to turn over thousands of Justice Department documents on **Fast & Furious**.

President Obama asserted Executive Privilege to try to protect Holder. But for Executive Privilege to apply, Obama would have had to have known about **Fast & Furious**, making the President as culpable as Holder.

Investigators suspect that Fast & Furious was an effort by the Obama Administration to discredit lawful gun ownership in America by purposefully creating gun crimes, thus inducing public outcry for gun control. When it put thousands of semi-automatic weapons in the hands of Mexican drug cartels, the Obama Justice Department knew these guns would be used to commit crimes, perhaps even kill some Americans. Then Obama could say: "See how dangerous these guns are. We must ban them."

9. "Federal Communications Commission (FCC): Regulated the Internet despite a court order from the Circuit Court of Appeals for Washington, D.C. stating that the FCC does not have the power to regulate the Internet." (SOURCE: Report from Nine State Attorneys General)

10. "Environmental Protection Agency (EPA): Imposed Cross-State Air Pollution Rules on the state of Texas at the last minute and without an opportunity for Texas to respond to the proposed regulation. EPA overreach was based on a dubious claim that air pollution from Texas affected a single air-quality monitor in Granite City, Illinois more than 500 miles and three states away from Texas." (SOURCE: Report from Nine State Attorneys General)

11. "Department of Justice (DOJ): Rejected state voter ID statutes that are similar to those already approved by the Supreme Court of the United States. DOJ ignored section 8 of the Voting Rights Act which calls for protections against voter fraud, and used section 5 to administratively block measures to protect the integrity of elections passed by state legislatures." (SOURCE: Report from Nine State Attorneys General)

12. "DOJ: In violation of 10th Amendment, sued to prevent Arizona from using reasonable measures to discourage illegal immigration within its borders. Arizona has a large number of illegal immigrants, compared to other states, and needs to be able to act to reduce the number." (SOURCE: Report from Nine State Attorneys General)

13. "DOJ: Went to court to stop enforcement of Alabama's immigration reform laws, which require collection of the immigration status of public school students, require businesses to use E-Verify, and prohibit illegal immigrants from receiving public benefits." (SOURCE: Report from Nine State Attorneys General)

14. "White House: Made "recess appointments" to the National Labor Relations Board and Consumer Financial Protection Bureau when Congress was NOT in recess. The Obama Administration has ignored the ruling by the D.C. Circuit Court of Appeals that the appointments are unconstitutional." (SOURCE: Report from Nine State Attorneys General)

15. "Equal Employment Opportunity Commission (EEOC): Interfered with a Michigan church's selection of its own ministers by trying to force the church to reinstate a minister who was discharged for her disagreement with the religious doctrine of the church." (SOURCE: Report from Nine State Attorneys General)

16. "Department of Energy (DOE): In 2009, the Obama Administration arbitrarily broke federal law, violated various contracts, and derailed the most studied energy project in American history at Yucca Mountain by denying it a license, thus costing the American people more than $31 billion." (SOURCE: Report from Nine State Attorneys General)

17. Department of the Interior (DOI): Forced Glendale, a family-oriented town in Arizona, to become another Las Vegas against its will by granting "reservation status" to a 54-acre plot in the town, where the Tohono O'odham Indian Nation plans to build a resort and casino." (SOURCE: Report from Nine State Attorneys General)

18. Without Congressional approval, Obama gutted the work requirement for welfare recipients passed by Congress and signed into law by President Bill Clinton.

19. In the bailout of General Motors and Chrysler, Obama illegally shortchanged bond holders in favor of Labor Unions, despite U.S. bankruptcy laws that specify that bond holders be first in line to be paid back.

20. Eager to use the killing of Osama bin Laden for political gain, Obama exposed the identity and method of operation of the Navy SEALs team that conducted the operation in Pakistan,

thus exposing its members to a lifetime of risk because they have been targeted for assassination by Islamists. A short time after Obama exposed the Navy SEALs' method of operation, 22 SEALs were shot down and killed in Afghanistan. It is a violation of law for the President or any American to reveal classified military secrets.

21. President Obama established an extra-constitutional top secret "kill list" of people (including Americans) who can be summarily killed on sight – presumably by drones -- without due process. Once on Obama's kill list, an American citizen can be targeted and executed on the opinion of a single government bureaucrat. That's not how our legal system is supposed to work.

22. Obama Administration officials twisted the arms of defense contractors to not issue layoff notices in October of 2012 so as to avoid causing bad news for Obama right before the election — even though federal law (the "WARN Act") requires such notices. ; Not only is this a violation of the WARN Act, it's also an unlawful use of federal officials for campaign purposes.

23. President Obama intervened militarily in Libya in 2011 without the Congressional approval required by the War Powers Act.

24. Obama knowingly lied to Congress and the American people about the killing of U.S. Ambassador Chris Stevens and three other Americans in Benghazi, Libya. The President and his representatives repeatedly said an anti-Islamic video sparked a spontaneous uprising in Libya that resulted in the killings even though Obama knew that the attack was a well-planned military-style assault by al Qaeda on the anniversary of September 11.

25. Michelle Obama's family trip to Africa in June of 2011, including a private safari at a South African game reserve, cost American taxpayers $424,000 for air travel alone. Mrs. Obama

brought along both her makeup artist and hairstylist, as well as her mother, a niece and nephew, and her daughters, who were listed as "senior staff members."

7
A LIST OF OBAMA'S CONSTITUTIONAL VIOLATIONS

Obama took the Presidential Oath, swearing to preserve, protect and defend the Constitution of the United States" but has: Used Executive Privilege in regards to Fast & Furious gun running scandal. When Government misconduct is the concern Executive privilege is negated.

23 Executive Orders on gun control – infringement of the 2nd Amendment

Executive Order bypassing Congress on immigration – Article 1 Section 1, ALL Legislative power held by Congress

NDAA – Section 1021. Due process Rights negated. Violation of 3rd, 4th, 5th, 6th, and 7th Amendments.

Executive Order 13603 NDRP – Government can seize anything

Executive Order 13524 – Gives INTERPOL jurisdiction on American soil beyond law enforcement agencies, including the FBI.

Executive Order 13636 Infrastructure Cybersecurity – Bypassing Congress Article 1 Section 1, ALL Legislative power held by Congress

Signed into law the establishment of NO Free Speech zones – noncompliance is a felony. Violation of 1st Amendment.

Attempt to tax political contributions – 1st Amendment

DOMA Law – Obama directed DOJ to ignore the Constitution and separation of powers and not enforce the law.

Dodd-Frank – Due process and separation of powers.

Consumer Financial Protection Bureau writing and interpreting law. Article. I. Section. 1

Drone strikes on American Citizens – 5th Amendment Due process Rights negated

Bypassed Congress and gave EPA power to advance Cap-n-Trade

Attempt for Graphic tobacco warnings (under appeal) – 1st Amendment

Four Exec. appointments – Senate was NOT in recess (Court has ruled unconstitutional yet the appointees still remain)

Appointing agency czars without the "advice and consent of the Senate." Violation of Article II, Section 2

Obama took Chairmanship of UN Security Council – Violation of Section 9.

Obamacare (ACA) mandate – SCOTUS had to make it a tax because there is no Constitutional authority for Congress to force Americans to engage in commerce.

Contraceptive, abortifacients mandate violation of First Ammendment

Healthcare waivers – No president has dispensing powers Refuses to acknowledge state's 10th Amendment rights to nullify Obamacare

Going after states (AZ lawsuit) for upholding Federal law (immigration) -10th Amendment.

Chrysler Bailout -TARP – violated creditors rights and bankruptcy law, as well as Takings and Due Process Clauses – 5th Amendment (G.W. Bush also illegally used TARP funds for bailouts)

The Independent Payment Advisory Board (appointees by the president). Any decisions by IPAB will instantly become law starting in 2014 – Separation of Powers, Article 1 Section 1.

Congress did not approve Obama's war in Libya. Article I, Section 8, First illegal war U.S. has engaged in. Impeachable under Article II, Section 4.

Obama falsely claims UN can usurp Congressional war powers.

Obama has acted outside the constitutional power given him – this in itself is unconstitutional.

With the approval of Obama, the NSA and the FBI are tapping directly into the servers of 9 internet companies to gain access to emails, video/audio, photos, documents, etc. This program is code named PRISM. NSA also collecting data on all phone calls in U.S. – Violation of 4th Amendment.

Plans to sign U.N. Firearms treaty – 2nd Amendment.

The Senate/Obama immigration bill (approved by both) raises revenue – Section 7. All Bills for raising Revenue shall originate in the House of Representatives;

Obama refuses to uphold the Business Mandate Law (ACA) for a year. President does not have that authority – Article. I. Section. 1. All legislative Powers herein granted shall be vested in a Congress of the United States. The president "shall take care that the laws be faithfully executed" -Article II, Section 3.

A Constitutional law professor (even their students) should know better. The TRUTH is Obama was a speaker not a law professor, and clearly he has not respected or protected the

Constitution. Obama has broken his oath to preserve, protect, and defend the Constitution of the United States. Article II, Section 1.

8

100 Ways Barack Obama
Is Just Like George W. Bush

The election of President Obama was in no small part, a referendum on the administration of George W. Bush, and his victory was interpreted as a sound rebuke to eight years of open ended warfare, a vast and growing police state, the destruction of civil liberties, disregard for the Constitution, unchecked executive power, lies and broken promises, hypocrisy and arrogance, a lack of transparency in government, out-of-control federal spending, fever-pitch fearmongering, rampant corruption, and some really stupid gaffes. But what have we gotten instead?

More of the same. A LOT more of the same. In fact, every negative aspect of the Bush Administration has come back with a vengeance in the presidency of Barack H. Obama. Everything the American people detested so strongly about Bush has not only characterized the presidency of his successor, it's gotten much worse. Don't believe me? The following is a list of 100 ways President Obama is just like President Bush. We might as well consider it a third Bush term on steroids, or call Mr. Obama "Bush 2.0." If you honestly didn't like Bush, you can't possibly justify liking Obama, not unless you ignore the facts:

Open Ended Warfare

One of the most disastrous and destructive aspects of the Bush Administration was a ramping up of the military-industrial complex to a level unprecedented in U.S. history. Bush's *Global War on Terror* worried critics because of its lack of clear objectives, no set timeline, and no specific enemy (as terror is a tactic, not an enemy). Along with it came the Bush Doctrine of preemptive warfare against countries that had not attacked the United States, which formed the foundation-- along with a few lies and sketchy intelligence-- for the massive, costly, and deadly war in Iraq.

The antiwar movement in America reached a fever pitch under President Bush, and rightly so, but has Obama put an end to this tragic era in American history? He could be forgiven if he had merely taken some time to draw down troops in the Middle East and abroad, but instead, within his first term Obama has actually taken Bush's war machine and put it in overdrive, sending significantly more troops to fight overseas, spending more money on "defense" than even Bush, and engaging the U.S. in even more conflicts on more fronts, sometimes even ignoring the Constitutional separation of powers (*i.e.* breaking the law) in order to pursue warfare on a level unmatched by the worst excesses of the Bush Administration:

1. Iraq - We should have known in 2008 that we wouldn't see any real change from the Obama Administration. Despite campaigning for the U.S. Senate in 2004 on a platform of voting against Bush's war budgets, when he became a Senator, Obama **voted for every single one** of Bush's requests to continue funding war in the Middle East. Apparently, his streak of broken promises started long before campaigning for the White House (and we'll get to those later down the list).

Then right off the bat in February of 2009, a mere month into his administration, President Obama **revealed** a phony withdrawal plan that would take three months longer than promised, and leave a whopping 50,000 troops in Iraq (out of the 135,000 that were there when Obama assumed office). Eight months later in October

2009, 131,000 troops remained in Iraq, and Obama sent another 1000 at the request of theater commanders in Iraq. Seriously.

1. **First Surge in Afghanistan** - Think Iraq was bad? It gets better! *Mr. (Blind) Hope and (Regime) Change kicked off* his presidency with a 17,000 troop surge to Afghanistan in February of 2009. 17,000! Don't defend him. Don't say it was necessary to help win the war there. You would not have defended Bush and you know it. Mr. Obama started his presidency by radically escalating Bush's war.

   3. Second Surge in Afghanistan - But wait- there's more! By December of 2009, less than a year into his presidency, Obama decided to outdo even himself and send another whopping *30,000* troops to Afghanistan! By this point, Al-Qaeda was scattered and devastated. Our troops were overseas fighting someone else's civil war, not defending our freedoms or our safety.

   4. Phony Afghan Withdrawal - In June of 2011, Obama announced a "troop withdrawal" from Afghanistan, and true to form, it was as phony as his Iraq withdrawal. Even if he stays on schedule and makes the most "radical" withdrawal on the table by the end of 2012-- 30,000 troops-- there would still be more than twice as many troops as there were in January 2009 when Obama took office. Only in the Orwellian world of U.S. foreign policy could something like that be called a withdrawal.

   5. The Rise of Drone Warfare - The Obama Administration's continued and extensive use of weaponized aerial drones to bomb enemy targets in countries throughout the Middle East (sometimes resulting in the deaths of dozens of civilians at a time when the drone operators or intelligence make a mistake) has touched off a drone arms race with the rest of the world, most notably China. Great. Just great.

6. Bombing Campaign in Yemen - Bush bombed in Yemen, but Obama's really been stepping it up.

7. Bombing Campaign in Somalia - In Somalia too!

8. Bombing Campaign in Pakistan - Under Obama, there have been more drone strikes in Pakistan than there ever were under Bush, and they're also claiming more civilians lives, Pakistanis claim, leading the country into uproar and protest against the United States.

9. Bombing Campaign in Libya - In March of 2011, President Obama took America to war in an entirely new country, Libya, taking sides with insurgents in a civil war against a dictator that Washington has supported for years up until now. Expanding Bush's old wars wasn't enough it would seem; Obama had to start some new ones of his own, against a country that had not attacked us and did not threaten us. And get this: in all likelihood, we've been fighting on the same side as Al-Qaeda in Libya's civil war!

10. Defense Spending Levels - "Defense" spending has only gone up during President Obama's first term from $616 billion under Bush in 2008 to $768 billion in 2011, and Obama still wantseven more. We were promised change. Why are we spending even more on bombs and bullets?

11. Record Casualty Levels - Under Obama, the wars

haven't just gotten bigger, more numerous, and even more legally dubious than under Bush (more on that later)-- they've gotten deadlier. According to the most up-to-date figures as of this publication, under Obama, the U.S. **casualty rate** in Afghanistan is *five times greater* than it was under Bush.

12. "Overseas Contingency Operations" - Despite ramping the Global War on Terror up to unprecedented levels as detailed above, the Obama Administration decided to seriously downplay its title by renaming it "Overseas Contingency Operations." Chillingly Orwellian, isn't it? And quite typically Obama: make no substantive changes at all (other than to make things worse and accelerate the damage done by Bush), but do make a big deal about changing a name or a logo!

13. God and War Rhetoric - To wrap up Obama's continuation of Bush's foreign policy, I give you none other than Jon Stewart, marveling at how similar Obama's war rhetoric is to Bush's, even to the point of invoking God in our fight against other countries, and "refusing to apologize" for our way of life (which apparently includes bombing everybody else):

THE VAST POLICE STATE

Bush critics consider his presidency to have inaugurated an era unprecedented in U.S. history for violations of civil liberties, privacy, and the constitutional amendments that protect Americans from unwarranted police actions by the government. The creation of a vast, "national security" state has alarmed critics as something more akin to fascist dictatorship than American republicanism. Yet all of Bush's worst and most tyrannical abuses have not only been continued by the Obama Administration, but taken to a whole new level:

14. The Patriot Act - A favorite target of Bush critics, the Patriot Act violates the 1st, 4th, and 5th amendments of the Constitution. Passed and renewed over and over again with little debate or deliberation, this gargantuan bill gave the federal government sweeping new powers to police its citizenry while ignoring the constitutional restrictions our Founding Fathers created to protect us from tyranny.

It should be no surprise that after the failed efforts of one honest Republican senator to prevent its passage, Obama renewed the Patriot Act (from across the Atlantic Ocean by autopen) as president-- he voted for its renewal as a senator. On one of the most important issues of our era, Obama is indistinguishable from Bush. He supports the (un)Patriot(ic) Act.

15. The TSA - Created by an act of Congress during the Bush Administration, and organized within the Department of Homeland Security, the TSA has been annoying and harassing passengers at airports for a decade now. But under President Obama, it has become more aggressive and oppressive than it ever was under Bush, with the installment of dozens of radiation-emitting "naked body scanners" throughout the country and directives from the DHS to use "enhanced" pat downs that many critics say amount to sexual assault. Under Bush, the TSA was merely annoying. Under Obama, it is horrifyingly out of control.

16. The War on Drugs - The decades-long "War on Drugs" has been a spectacular failure of public policy, resulting in billions of wasted dollars, record levels of incarceration, higher rates of drug fatalities, and the creation of a violent international criminal drug cartel that thrives on continued prohibition. The 2009 Ogden Memo signaled that Obama might change course in the failed "War on Drugs." Nope. In July 2011, the Justice Department published a new memo indicating that things would stay just the same as they were under George W. Bush.

17. CIA Rendition - The CIA's "extraordinary rendition" program consists of seizing "terror suspects," detaining them without warrant or trial, and sending them offshore to outsource their "interrogation" to third world countries where they are tortured for information and confessions. Seriously. Torture was one of the big criticisms faced by the Bush Administration, and in February 2009, the Obama Administration wasted no time in quietly retaining the practice of rendition.

18. *Habeas Corpus* - The Obama Administration also continued Bush's suspension of the long-standing legal tradition of *habeas corpus*, insisting that it has the right to detain suspected terrorists indefinitely without trial.

19. You Do Not Have The Right To Remain Silent - The Obama Administration actually had the gall to ask "the Supreme Court to overrule long-standing law that stops police from initiating questions unless a defendant's lawyer is present, another stark example of the White House seeking to limit rather than expand rights."

20. ...or Test Genetic Evidence Used Against You -The Obama Administration has also limited "the rights of prisoners to test genetic evidence used to convict them."

21. The DHS and Swine Flu - The Obama Administration further empowered the growing police state and set a chilling precedent when it let the Department of Homeland Security manage a health issue, a strain of flu referred to as "swine flu." the DHS declared a state of emergency in the U.S. and got out in front of the (manufactured) swine flu "crisis."

DISREGARD FOR THE CONSTITUTION

AND UNCHECKED EXECUTIVE POWER

President Bush will be forever remembered by critics for his "imperial presidency," his usurpation of power from the other branches of government in violation of the Constitution. Instead of a nation guided by laws, under Bush our country descended even further into the lawless anarchy of executive tyranny, unchecked by the other branches of government and unrestrained by the Constitution. An autocrat, Bush did as he pleased, whether the law permitted it or not. Obama has been No different, Actually, he's been worse:

22. Faith-Based Initiatives - Obama curiously continued Bush's unconstitutional faith-based initiatives (ever heard of the First Amendment?).

23. Signing Statements - On the campaign trail, Obama calledpresidential "signing statements" (letters of interpretation and recommendations attached to Congressional legislation) unconstitutional and promised not to use them... then attached a signing statement to a $410 billion spending bill as president. If you want to know why this is a dangerous usurpation of power by the executive, click that first link above and Obama will it explain it to you himself. This also counts as a broken promise, which you'll read plenty more of soon.

24. Hillary Clinton Appointment - Unconstitutional. If you think I'm splitting hairs, you can bite me.

25 War in Libya - We already touched on this as one of Obama's expansions to Bush's open-ended warfare, but I didn't mention one key thing: this was was completely unconstitutional. Obama went to war in Libya without a formal declaration from Congress-- without even consulting Congress-- and according to both the War Powers Resolution and the U.S. Constitution itself, it is only the people's representatives in Congress that can take our nation to war, not the president alone.

Even Obama's own defense secretary said that America faced no imminent threat from Libya. Here are Obama's own words on the matter back when he was a senator:

"The President does not have power under the Constitution to unilaterally authorize a military attack in a situation that does not involve stopping an actual or imminent threat to the nation."

26. **Czars** - One significant change that will forever characterize the Obama administration is its radical and unprecedented expansion of a policy that started in the Nixon administration-- the unconstitutional appointment of "czars" as "principle officers" of policy within the administration who answer solely to the president without the advice and consent of Congress. By most recent estimates, Obama has appointed 41 of these "czars" to high level posts within his administration.

It is exactly this kind of centralization of executive power, isolated from the advice, consent, and oversight of the people via their representatives that worried Democrats about President George W.

Bush. Before he died, even the Democrats' most senior senator, Robert Byrd, condemned Obama "czar strategy" as an unprecedented and illegal power grab that centralizes power in the executive, evades congressional oversight, and violates the separation of powers required by law in the Constitution.

27. Distribution of TARP funds - Though you'll read about several broken promises in a minute, one promise Obama has kept is his distribution of TARP II funds to non-financialinstitutions, which is contrary to the stated intention of thosefunds in the legislation passed by Congress, making his action *illegal* *,unconstitutional*, and an expansion of unlimited executive power.

28. Converting federal loans to common stock - In a sneaky, underhanded, unconstitutional power play, Obamamoved to convert U.S. Federal loans to banking institutions into common stock, effectively *nationalizing* major portions of the U.S. banking industry.

29. Health provisions in the stimulus bill - Though hardly mentioned by the news media, the health provisions in the 2009 stimulus package passed by Obama represent a giant leap towards fascist medicine in this country. Details here.

30. Census Bureau Grab - Obama's move of the United States Census out of the Department of Commerce and under the direct control of the *White House* was unconstitutional, politically motivated, and a dangerous, *undemocratic* expansion of executive power.

31. Forcing US banks to accept TARP money - What's worse than bailing out wealthy banks with money taken from poor and middle class Americans? Forcing wealthy banks to take the bailout money against their will.

32. Rebuking SCOTUS - This was extremely unusual and entirely unseemly for a President of the United States to do during a State of the Union Address.

LIES AND BROKEN PROMISES

Lies, lies, lies. The Bush Administration was marred by lies and broken campaign promises. His administration looked

nothing likethe promises he made during the 2000 Presidential Campaign. The Obama Administration has been no different.

33. Non-Emergency Legislation - Obama promised to "publish all non-emergency legislation to the website for five days... before the President signs it," then broke that promise over and over again. (This is also a big transparency problem... more of those later.)

34. Lobbyists - Despite promising to keep lobbyists out of his administration, Obama broke his word again and again (making 17 exceptions to this promise in his first two weeks as president).

35. Income Tax Cuts for Seniors - Obama promised to eliminate income taxation for seniors making less than $50,000 a year. He has broken this promise despite numerous opportunities to keep it, including the economic stimulus package and his administration's first budget proposal.

36. Tax Credit for Businesses - The President also boasted during his campaign that "During 2009 and 2010, existing businesses will receive a $3,000 refundable tax credit for each additional full-time employee hired," and has failed to keep his word.

37. Retirement Accounts - Obama made it part of his agenda to "allow withdrawals of 15% up to $10,000 from retirement accounts without penalty (although subject to the normal taxes). This would apply to withdrawals in 2008 (including retroactively) and 2009," but didn't include this measure in the stimulus package or his budget proposal.

38. The Armenian Genocide - Obama broke his promise to recognize the *Armenian Genocide*.

39. Tax Credit for College Tuition - On the campaign trail, Obama promised a $4000 tax credit for college tuition, but backpedaled when he signed a much smaller $2,500 college tax credit into law.

40. The Partisan Tenor - Obama promised a different tone in Washington D.C. and a move past bitter, *partisan* rhetoric. It took him less than a week as president to berate *Republicans* and sully the dignity of his office by picking a very public rhetorical fightwith a private citizen, *Rush Limbaugh*.

41. Dog-Gone Lies - If you can't trust someone with little things, you certainly can't trust them with bigger things.

Obama chose purebred dog, "Bo" for the White House family's "first dog" instead of adopting a dog from a shelter like he promised.

42. Spinning the Auto Bailout - Someone explain to me again why a supposedly "progressive" president is lying to justify a coerced (and illegal) loan to a wealthy, irresponsible corporation from hard working poor and middle class Americans?

43. Taxing Some Employee Health Benefits - "The Obama administration is signaling to Congress that the president could support taxing some employee health benefits, as several influential lawmakers and many economists favor, to help pay for overhauling the health care system. The proposal is politically problematic for President Obama, however, since it is similar to one he denounced in the presidential campaign as 'the largest middle-class tax increase in history."

ARROGANCE AND HYPOCRISY

What got critics so especially emotional in their opposition to George W. Bush was not merely his demolition job of liberty and rule of law in America, but the cowboy arrogance and shameless hypocrisy that characterized his administration. Let's see if Obama has been any better:

44. "I won." - In his first private meeting with Congressional Republicans, instead of "reaching across the aisle" and seeking earnest dialogue, Obama smugly told them that he should have his way because "I won."

45. "Don't think we're not keeping score." - Obama to Rep. Peter DeFazio, one of the Democratic congressman who voted against the stimulus package, "Don't think we're not keeping score, brother."

46. I'm smart. You're dumb. - I'm smart. You're dumb. I'm right. You're wrong. Shut up and take it. That's pretty much what Obama said when asked about public opinion against raising the debt ceiling.

47. OBL Death - Just watch this video comparing President Bush's announcement after Hussein's capture to President Obama's announcement after Osama bin Laden's death. Notice a difference? Even Bush wasn't this arrogant, and that's saying something.

48. Schooled in Hypocrisy - Obama's daughters attend a private school in Washington D.C., enjoying the freedom of educational choice that the Obama Administration has denied to poor children who live in Washington (more on that later... when you read it, you're going to flip your lid).

49. Golf - In just "ten months as U.S. President, Mr Obama has already played as much golf as George W Bush did in his entire eight years in power."

50. "Mostly basketball." - It's crap like this.

51. Inauguration Footprint - Despite claiming our environment is in a state of crisis, Obama's extravagant inauguration alone emitted over 500 million pounds of CO2.

52. Inauguration Price - Obama's lavish inauguration also cost a whopping $170 million. (This is the same man who said: "There is no doubt that we've been living beyond our means and we're going to have to make some adjustments.")

53. Thermostat - After saying "We can't drive our SUVs and eat as much as we want and keep our homes on 72 degrees at all times... and then just expect that every country is going to say okay," journalists discovered that Obama cranks the thermostat in the Oval Office.

54. Earth Day Flights - Obama's Earth Day flights burned more than 9,000 gallons of fuel.

55. The Race Card - In 2009, Obama said: "we have to get to the point where we can have a conversation about big, important issues that matter to the American people without vitriol, without name-calling, without the assumption of the worst in other people's motives." Then in 2011, we learned that Obama has assumed the worst about the Tea Party's motives: they're racists.

56. AIG Bailout - AIG's second biggest campaign donation beneficiary: Barack Obama, who acted angry about the results of a bailout he helped to craft as U.S. Senator.

57. The Blame Game - Throughout his presidency, Obama has blamed Bush and stifled criticism by saying he inherited a mess from his predecessor. As you read through this list, however, can't you see how that might be a little bit hypocritical? Blame Bush for the wars while ramping them up and even starting new ones? Blame Bush for the deficit while spending even more than Bush did? Blame Bush for everything, while just making things worse?

LACK OF TRANSPARENCY

A common theme throughout Barack Obama's 2008 presidential campaign was transparency. Supporters wanted to see an administration that would restore some of the transparency in government that was lost during the Bush years. Unfortunately, Obama didn't deliver:

58. Closed door stimulus meetings - Within the first month of the Obama Administration, the country was rushed into accepting a multi-billion dollar stimulus package that was debated in secret, behind closed doors. The bill itself was too big for any of the congressmen themselves, much less the American people, to have an opportunity to actually read it. Then it was not published to the White House website for five days before Obama signed it despite his campaign promise to do so.

59. Closed door health care meetings (C-SPAN) - Despite Obama's promise to televise the health care debate on C-SPAN, the debate and ultimate passage of the "ObamaCare" bill happened without a public debate, behind closed doors, in secret meetings. More broken promises. Less transparency.

60. HHS "Transparency" - President Obama's rationing czar, who controls the health care of 1 in 3 Americans and has a budget larger than the freaking Pentagon's refuses to answer questions, grant interviews, or testify before Congress.

61. DC Voucher Program - The Obama Administration ended funding for Washington D.C.'s school voucher program, whilesuppressing a study that showed it delivered better results at a lower cost. Less transparency, lower quality education, and higher costs. Brilliant.

62. Prisoner Abuse Photos - In 2010 watchdog group,*OpenTheGovernment.org* found that the Obama Administration, following in the steps of the Bush Administration, continued to block the release of photos depicting prisoner abuse by American troops in Iraq and Afghanistan

63. State Secrets Privilege and CIA torture - The same group also noted that Obama's administration continued to invoke the state secrets privilege in cases involving alleged CIA torture.

64. Declassifications Drop - Further, they found that in 2009, fewer pages (28.8 million) were declassified governmentwide and the declassification rate fell significantly—from 61% of all material reviewed in 2008 to 55% in 2009.

65. Only one question - After the Department of Homeland Security circulated a memo to state police departments warning of "right-wing" terrorism, Secretary Janet Napolitano did an interview, but would only answer **one question** with no follow ups about the memo.

66. Tax Returns!!! - Always focusing on appearances, never substantive changes, Obama made **a big flashy deal** out of releasing the President's and Vice President's income tax returns (oooohh- transparency!), which every President has done for years now. The embarrassing thing is, the Obamas were **totally shown up by the Bushes**-- according to their respective tax returns, the Obamas gave 6.5% of their 2008 income to charity while the Bushes gave 23% of theirs to charity in 2007.

67. Most Anti-Leak Administration Ever - The Obama Administration has **proven** far more aggressive than the Bush Administration in seeking to punish whistle-blowers within the administration.

OUT OF CONTROL SPENDING

Especially during the debt ceiling debate that raged all Summer of 2011, Democrats were quick to point out the "balanced budgets" of the Clinton years. Many of Bush's critics excoriated him for wrecking America's fiscal solvency and running up federal budget deficits unprecedented in U.S. history. It was completely irresponsible. MoveOn.org even made a famous ad showing children working in factories before posing the question: "Guess who's going to pay for Bush's deficits?"

Guess who's going to pay for Obama's even bigger deficits? Those same future generations of children:

68. Spending WAY MORE than Bush - Yeah, Bush's deficits were bad. But if you really believe that, you've got to be willing to condemn Obama's even bigger deficits. Here's a pretty good lookwith some hard figures at just how the two presidents compare. Bush was bad. Obama has been much worse.

69. Earmarks - Obama did a shameless 180 degree turn on earmarks by sharply criticizing them (and bragging that he would pass legislation without a single one) and then signing a spending bill with literally thousands of them.

70. Stimulus Package - There went $800 billion in productive capital right down the drain.

71. Health Care Bill - Another $900 billion.

72. TARP - I know this passed while Bush was president. But guess which then-senator gets some of the blame too because he voted to send it across Bush's desk? Barack Obama. $700 billion. Gosh, all these hundreds of billions add up to trillions real fast!

73. Bailing out Greece - Meanwhile, as America faces a fiscal crisis in 2011 because of all the aforementioned spending bills in 2008 - 2009, Obama thinks we have enough money to bailout another country halfway around the world.

74. Appointing Ben Bernanke - Another continuation of Bush era economics, fiscal policy, and monetary policy: Obama'sappointment of Ben Bernanke to another term as Fed Chair. Are you convinced that Mr. Obama is not so different from Mr. Bush yet?

75. Measly $100 million "cut" - But remember, this is Obama, so he's got to keep up appearances, which is why he made a big show of challenging his cabinet to cut a measly $100 million from the Federal budget (a .0027% cut in Federal spending... also, he admitted that this doesn't even represent a spending cut by saying that it will free up more money for Federal spending on other things like health and education).

FEAR MONGERING

One of the worst aspects of the Bush Administration (and a complicit media) was its use of fearmongering and panic to scare the American people into accepting its relentless march on our freedoms. In 2008, people clamored for a reasoned voice of hope. Instead, they got Obama:

76. Stimulus Package - Shrill: "If nothing is done, this recession could linger for years. The unemployment rate could reach double digits. For every day we wait or point fingers or drag our feet, more Americans will lose their jobs. More families will lose their savings. More dreams will be deferred and denied. And our nation will sink deeper into a crisis that, at some point, we may not be able to reverse."

77. Valentine's Day Vacation -And we know it was just fearmongering, because if Obama had meant the above words in earnest, then after passage of the stimulus act, he would not have taken off on a ritzy **Valentine's Day vacation** in Chicago for the weekend instead of signing the stimulus bill that he said needed to be passed as soon as possible to avert an irreversible *economic meltdown*. Also file this one under hypocrisy and lies.

78. Debt Ceiling - Obama knew full well that he was lying and fearmongering when he **said** that he could not guarantee Social Security checks would make it out to their beneficiaries if the debt limit wasn't raised by August 2nd. Without borrowing money, the federal government takes in $200 billion in receivables each month, plenty enough to service interest on the national debt, write Social Security checks, and continue military operations.

79. Health Care Bill - If you'll remember with me, the level of panicked rhetoric over health care in this country was at a fever pitch during the months leading up to passage of this bill. Along with the sanctimony, the secrecy, the backroom deals, the sudden changes in votes, the lack of public support, the narrow margin of passage, the size of the bill itself, and the fact that no one had actually read it before voting on it, the storyline was no different from passage of Bush's Medicare Part D (which many Democrats opposed).

80. DHS Memo - This shrill gem published in the early days of the Obama Administration **instructed** state police departments that both active and inactive US military personnel are potential domestic terrorists, comparing them to Timothy McVeigh and

Terry Nichols. Additional potential terrorists, according to the memo, included Tea Party protesters, anyone who vocally supports the amendments in the Bill of Rights, and anyone who is vocally pro-life.

81. Swine Flu - Jon Stewart says it best.

82. Patriot Act Renewal -It was the same old line used by the Bush Administration. We need these tools to deal with the terrorists. If we don't renew the Patriot Act, America will be less safe. Blah blah blah blah blah. Then after renewing it, of course the administration continues bombing other countries and we wonder why there are terrorists out there targeting Americans and why we feel less safe.

CORRUPTION

I'll try to make this quick for you:

83. Joe Sestak - Rep. Joe Sestak (D-PA) was (illegally) offered a job by the Obama administration in exchange for dropping out of the senatorial primary against Obama supporter Sen. Arlen Specter. And Sestak's not the only one. (Proof.)

84. Tim Geithner - Obama appointed Tim Geithner to the office of Secretary of the Treasury, even though he was a part of the problem with the economic *status quo* and evaded his taxes for years.

85. Annette Nazareth - Obama also selected Annette Nazareth for the position of Deputy Treasury Secretary, who withdrew after a month long probe into her taxes.

86. Tom Daschle - Next there's Tom Daschle, appointed by Obama to the Department of Health and Human Services. He had to resign his nomination for the position **because of tax evasion**.

87. Nancy Killefer - Obama also appointed Nancy Killefer for Chief Performance Officer, but she had to step down because-- SURPRISE-- **she didn't pay her taxes either!**

88. Rahm Emmanuel - There's also Rahm Emmanuel, who served as Chief of Staff even though he **failed to report** five years of free rent at a U.S. Congressman's property in accordance with IRS policy and congressional ethics rules.

89. Louis Susman - "Barack Obama has been **embroiled in a cronyism row** after reports that he intends to make Louis Susman, one of his biggest fundraisers, the new US ambassador in London. The selection of Mr. Susman, a lawyer and banker from the president's hometown of Chicago, rather than an experienced diplomat, raises new questions about Mr Obama's commitment to the special relationship with Britain."

90. Adolfo Carrion - Adolfo Carrion, Director of White House Office of Urban Affairs, "**pocketed thousands** of dollars in campaign cash from city developers whose projects he approved or funded with taxpayers' money."

91. "GunGate" - **Obama's** Iran-Contra scandal?

REALLY STUPID GAFFES

Who could forget **Bush's gaffes**? While the rest of the world rejoiced at Obama's inauguration, comedians were secretly a little disappointed. For eight years, Bush made such an easy target. Lucky for them, Obama has had plenty moments of his own:

92. Bowing - In 2009, President Obama actually bowed to a foreign monarch, King Abdullah. After a few more bowing gaffes like bowing to Japanese Emperor Akihito, it started getting weird when Obama bowed to the mayor of Tampa:

93. Lamest Gift Ever - At their first meeting, U.K. Prime Minister Gordon Brown's gift to Obama: "an ornamental pen holder made from the timbers of the Victorian anti-slave ship HMS Gannet," and "a framed commission for HMS Resolute and a first edition of the seven-volume biography of Churchill by Sir Martin Gilbert." Obama's gift to Brown: a box set of 25 classic American DVDs... that don't work on European DVD players. Fail.

94. England =/= UK - To make matters worse, Obama used "England" to denote the U.K. -a gaffe that people from Scotland, Ireland, and Wales don't appreciate and chalk up to American ignorance and parochialism.

95. Thanking Himself - And check out Obama thanking himselffor being invited to speak with the Irish Prime Minister because he was having teleprompter troubles.

96. Arguing with a teleprompter - And it only gets better: behold the bizarre spectacle of the President "arguing with" a teleprompter during a speech.

97. Special Olympics - Yikes, Barack: "I've been practicing bowling. I bowled a 129. It was like the Special Olympics or something." -Obama on *The Tonight Show*

98. All 57 states! - This one is sooo Bush-like.

99. Terrorizing NYC - Post 9-11, this is about the least sensitive, most stupid thing you could do: Airforce 1 panics New York City residents with extremely low flight plan for photo op and no public announcement.

100. Gulf Oil Spill - Okay, this one isn't really a gaffe, just a long nightmare for everybody that lasted all summer back in 2010. It didn't really fit into any of the other categories, but this wasObama's Katrina for sure. That oil just kept flowing, and Obama just kept golfing.

CONCLUSION

Anybody who voted for Obama want to fess up and admit they made a mistake?

12 IMPEACHABLE OFFENSES

THE LIST IS QUITE LONG AND I'VE SEEN UP TO 57 AREAS THAT SUGGEST HIGH CRIMES AND MISDEMEANORS HAVE BEEN COMMITTED BY THE CURRENT OCCUPANT OF 1600 PENNSYLVANIA AVE.

I WILL LIMIT MY NUMBER TO 12, SIMPLY BECAUSE IMPEACHMENT WOULD BE A FRUITLESS EXERCISE, THE U.S. SENATE IS HELD BY THE DEMOCRATS, AND THEY ARE UNLIKELY TO VOTE TO CONVICT THE CHOSEN ONE.

WHAT IS NEEDED IS A WATERGATE TYPE SPECIAL COUNSEL, WITH NO TIES TO THE GOVERNMENT AND THEN BRING HIM TO TRIAL OVER HIS LIES, ENCOURAGING MEMBERS OF HIS TEAM TO LIE, WHILE DOING NOTING BUT OBSTRUCT JUSTICE ON BENGHAZI.

1. PRESIDENT OBAMA HAS APPOINTED NUMEROUS PEOPLE TO CABINET LEVEL POSITIONS WITHOUT THE ADVICE AND CONSENT OF THE U.S. SENATE, AS IS REQUIRED BY THE CONSTITUTION. THESE INDIVIDUALS ARE GIVEN EXTRAORDINARY POWER AND INDEPENDENT FUNDING, AND ARE NOT UNDER THE SCRUTINY OF CONGRESS. THE FACT THAT OBAMA CALLS THEM CZARS DOES NOT MAKE THEM LEGAL.

2. THE PUSH BY PRES. OBAMA TO PASS HEALTH CARE LEGISLATION IN THE CONGRESS OF THE UNITED STATES THAT HE WAS FULLY AWARE WAS UNCONSTITUTIONAL. HE HAS CONTINUED TO USE HIS POWERS AND EXECUTIVE BRANCH OF GOVERNMENT

TO IMPLEMENT THIS LEGISLATION DESPITE THE FACT THAT A FEDERAL JUDGE HAS DECLARED THE ENTIRE LAW UNCONSTITUTIONAL, AND ORDERED THAT IT NOT BE IMPLEMENTED.

3. DESPITE THE FACT THAT THE UNITED STATES SENATE REFUSED TO PASS THE CAP AND TRADE BILL, THE PRESIDENT HAS ORDERED THE ENVIRONMENTAL PROTECTION AGENCY TO USE REGULATIONS TO IMPLEMENT KEY PORTIONS OF THE BILL, INCLUDING THOSE REGULATING SO-CALLED GREENHOUSE GASES. OBAMA HIMSELF HAS ACKNOWLEDGED THAT THIS WILL FORCE ENERGY PRICES IN THIS COUNTRY TO SKYROCKET. HE IS TAKING THESE ACTIONS IN DIRECT DEFIANCE OF THE WILL OF THE PEOPLE OF THE UNITED STATES, THE WILL OF CONGRESS, AND THE CONSTITUTION.

4. THROUGH THE DEPARTMENT OF THE INTERIOR OBAMA HAS PLACED A MORATORIUM ON OFFSHORE OIL DRILLING OR EXPLORATION OFF BOTH THE ATLANTIC AND PACIFIC COASTS OF THE UNITED STATES AND IN PARTS OF THE GULF OF MEXICO. HE IS ALSO PROHIBITED NEW DRILLING EXPLORATION IN ANY STATES IN THE UNITED STATES. THESE ACTIONS BY THE DEPARTMENT OF INTERIOR HAVE CONTINUED IN DIRECT DEFIANCE OF SEVERAL COURT ORDERS ISSUED BY A FEDERAL JUDGE IN NEW ORLEANS, LOUISIANA THE DECLARED THAT THE DEPARTMENT HAD NO AUTHORITY TO ISSUE SUCH A MORATORIUM. IN FACT THE SECRETARY OF THE DEPARTMENT OF THE INTERIOR HAS BEEN HELD IN CONTEMPT BY THE SAME JUDGE.

5. INSTEAD OF ALLOWING AMERICAN COMPANIES TO DRILL FOR OIL DOMESTICALLY, OBAMA HAS BETRAYED THE AMERICAN PEOPLE AND AUTHORIZED LOANS OF BILLIONS OF DOLLARS TO COUNTRIES LIKE BRAZIL AND MEXICO SO THAT THEY CAN DRILL FOR OIL, AND THEN SELL THAT OIL TO THE UNITED STATES. THIS WILL DRAMATICALLY INCREASE OUR DEPENDENCE ON FOREIGN NATIONS SUCH AS VENEZUELA, BRAZIL, SAUDI ARABIA, AND EVEN LIBYA THAT DO NOT SERVE THE INTEREST OF AMERICA OR THE AMERICAN PEOPLE.

6. PRESIDENT OBAMA HAS ABDICATED HIS RESPONSIBILITY TO ENFORCE THE LAWS OF THE UNITED STATES AGAINST ILLEGAL IMMIGRATION. HE HAS VIRTUALLY DECLARED OUR SOUTHERN BORDER AN OPEN BORDER BY DECLARING CERTAIN AREAS OF FEDERAL LAND IN STATES LIKE ARIZONA AS OFF-LIMITS TO FEDERAL, STATE, AND LOCAL AUTHORITIES. THIS IS DESPITE THE FACT THAT THESE AREAS ARE BEING USED TO BRING IN THOUSANDS OF ILLEGAL IMMIGRANTS, MASSIVE AMOUNTS OF DRUGS, AND ALSO BEING USED BY FOREIGN TERRORISTS TO INFILTRATE THE UNITED STATES. HE HAS ALSO ORDERED THE BORDER PATROL NOT TO ARREST MOST ILLEGAL IMMIGRANTS ENTERING THE COUNTRY, AND HAS STOPPED DEPORTATION PROCEEDINGS AGAINST THOUSANDS OF PEOPLE IN THIS COUNTRY ILLEGALLY. HE IS BYPASSING THE CONGRESS OF THE UNITED STATES WHICH HAS SOLE AUTHORITY OVER IMMIGRATION MATTERS.

7. THE PRESIDENT AND HIS ATTY. GEN. ERIC HOLDER HAVE CLEARLY VIOLATED THEIR OATH OF OFFICE BY

JOINING WITH FOREIGN COUNTRIES IN A LAWSUIT AGAINST THE SOVEREIGN STATE OF ARIZONA TO STOP IT FROM ENFORCING THE FEDERAL IMMIGRATION LAWS.

8. PRESIDENT OBAMA HAS ORDERED THE FEDERAL COMMUNICATIONS COMMISSION TO ADOPT REGULATIONS GIVING THE FEDERAL GOVERNMENT CONTROL OF THE INTERNET AND ITS CONTENTS, INCLUDING PROVIDING OBAMA WITH A KILL SWITCH THAT GIVES HIM AUTHORITY TO SHUT DOWN THE INTERNET IF HE SEES FIT. THIS IS IN DIRECT VIOLATION OF A DECISION BY THE UNITED STATES SUPREME COURT THAT THE FCC HAS NO CONSTITUTIONAL AUTHORITY TO CONTROL THE INTERNET.

9. ONE OF THE PARAMOUNT RESPONSIBILITIES OF THE PRESIDENT OF THE UNITED STATES AND HIS EXECUTIVE BRANCH OF GOVERNMENT IS TO ENFORCE AND DEFEND LAWS ADOPTED BY CONGRESS UNLESS THEY ARE DECLARED UNCONSTITUTIONAL BY THE UNITED STATES SUPREME COURT. OBAMA HAS DECIDED THAT HE SHOULD IGNORE THIS CONSTITUTIONAL MANDATE, AND THAT AS PRESIDENT HE IS MORE POWERFUL THAN EITHER THE CONGRESS OF THE UNITED STATES OR THE SUPREME COURT. HE HAS UNILATERALLY DECLARED THAT THE DEFENSE OF MARRIAGE ACT PASSED BY THE CONGRESS IS UNCONSTITUTIONAL, AND FURTHER DECLARED THAT HE WILL NOT HAVE THE JUSTICE DEPARTMENT DEFEND IT AGAINST LAWSUITS. HE HAS ESSENTIALLY SAID THAT HE IS THE SUPREME RULER OF THE UNITED STATES, AND THAT THE CONGRESS AND THE FEDERAL JUDICIARY ARE IRRELEVANT.

10. IT HAS RECENTLY BEEN LEARNED THAT ACTING THROUGH THE BUREAU OF ALCOHOL, TOBACCO, AND FIREARMS THE OBAMA ADMINISTRATION HAS BEEN INVOLVED FOR THE PAST SEVERAL MONTHS IN GETTING LEGITIMATE AND LAW-ABIDING GUN STORE OWNERS ALONG OUR SOUTHERN BORDER TO SUPPLY WEAPONS TO STRAW BUYERS THAT THE GOVERNMENT KNEW WOULD DELIVER THEM TO THE DRUG CARTELS IN MEXICO. THIS WAS BILLED AS A STING OPERATION AGAINST THE CARTELS WHEN IN FACT IT WAS DESIGNED TO PRODUCE FRAUDULENT DATA SHOWING THAT LARGE NUMBERS OF WEAPONS WERE GOING FROM THE UNITED STATES TO THE MEXICAN DRUG DEALERS. THIS DATA WAS THEN TO BE USED, AND IS BEING USED, TO TRY TO JUSTIFY NEW GUN CONTROL REGULATIONS TO LIMIT THE RIGHTS OF AMERICAN CITIZENS TO KEEP AND BEAR ARMS. IT HAS NOTHING TO DO WITH ARRESTING MEMBERS OF THE DRUG OPERATIONS. THE ADMINISTRATION HAS, IN EFFECT, ARMED OUR ENEMIES, AND ONE BORDER PATROL AGENT HAS ALREADY BEEN KILLED BY ONE OF THESE WEAPONS. NOW, HE INTENDS TO IMPOSE GUN CONTROL LAWS BY EXECUTIVE ORDER SO HE WILL NOT HAVE TO DEAL WITH CONGRESS.

11. THE PRESIDENT OF THE UNITED STATES IS NOT AUTHORIZED BY THE CONSTITUTION TO TAKE OUR NATION TO WAR WITHOUT THE CONSENT OF THE CONGRESS OF THE UNITED STATES. THE ONLY EXCEPTION TO THIS IS THE AUTHORITY GRANTED TO THE PRESIDENT BY CONGRESS UNDER THE WAR POWERS ACT. THIS LAW ALLOWS THE PRESIDENT TO TAKE IMMEDIATE ACTION WITHOUT THE CONSENT OF CONGRESS IF THERE IS AN IMMINENT THREAT TO THE

SECURITY OF THE UNITED STATES, OR ITS CITIZENS. ALTHOUGH THERE WAS CLEARLY NO SUCH IMMINENT THREAT CAUSED BY THE CIVIL WAR IN LIBYA, THE PRESIDENT COMMITTED MEMBERS OF THE UNITED STATES MILITARY TO COMBAT MISSIONS IN A FOREIGN COUNTRY WITHOUT THE CONSENT OF CONGRESS. HE BASED HIS AUTHORITY ON A UNITED NATIONS RESOLUTION, AND A RESOLUTION BY THE ARAB LEAGUE.

12. LAST BUT NOT THE LEAST, OF MY DIRTY DOZEN OF IMPEACHABLE OFFENSES, IS THE FACT THAT SINCE TAKING OFFICE THE PRESIDENT HAS USED EXECUTIVE ORDERS, LAWS PUSHED THROUGH CONGRESS IN THE DARK OF NIGHT, AND ADMINISTRATIVE ACTIONS BY HIS DEPARTMENTS TO NATIONALIZE AND CONTROL AUTOMOBILE MANUFACTURERS, BANKS, INSURANCE COMPANIES, AND PORTIONS OF THE HEALTHCARE INDUSTRY. THIS IS DESIGNED TO TAKE OUR COUNTRY FROM A FREE ENTERPRISE ECONOMY TO A SOCIALIST ECONOMY. THERE IS ABSOLUTELY NO AUTHORITY IN THE CONSTITUTION OF TE UNITED STATES THAT ALLOWS THE PRESIDENT TO DO THIS.

ARTICLE II, SECTION 4 OF THE CONSTITUTION PROVIDES AS FOLLOWS:

"THE PRESIDENT, VICE PRESIDENT AND ALL CIVIL OFFICERS OF THE UNITED STATES SHALL BE REMOVED FROM OFFICE ON IMPEACHMENT FOR, AND CONVICTION OF, TREASON, BRIBERY, OR OTHER HIGH CRIMES AND MISDEMEANORS."

I CONTEND THAT AMONG THOSE HIGH CRIMES AND MISDEMEANORS IS THE INTENTIONAL VIOLATION OF THE OATH OF OFFICE ADMINISTERED TO THE PRESIDENT AND ALL OTHER FEDERAL OFFICIALS. IN FACT, FEDERAL LAW AT 5 U.S.C. 7311 SPECIFICALLY PROVIDES THAT VIOLATION OF THE OATH OF OFFICE INCLUDES ADVOCATING THE OVERTHROWING OF OUR CONSTITUTIONAL FORM OF GOVERNMENT. THIS IS SPECIFICALLY DECLARED A CRIMINAL OFFENSE IN 18 U.S.C. 1918 AND IS PUNISHABLE BY BOTH A FINE AND IMPRISONMENT.

IN THE 12 AREAS I MENTIONED IN THE PARAGRAPHS ABOVE I FIRMLY BELIEVE THAT OBAMA, ERIC HOLDER, AND NUMEROUS OTHER MEMBERS OF HIS ADMINISTRATION HAVE GONE BEYOND JUST ADVOCATING THE OVERTHROW OF OUR CONSTITUTIONAL FORM OF GOVERNMENT. THEY ARE ACTUALLY ENGAGED IN MAKING IT HAPPEN, AND AS A RESULT SHOULD BE IMPEACHED AND CONVICTED.

WILL THERE BE AN IMPEACHMENT AND CONVICTION IN THE CURRENT CONGRESS? PROBABLY NOT, SINCE IT TAKES A TWO THIRDS VOTE IN THE HOUSE OF REPRESENTATIVES TO IMPEACH, AND A TWO THIRDS VOTE IN THE SENATE TO CONVICT. WITH HARRY REID AND THE PROGRESSIVES STILL IN CONTROL OF THE SENATE, AND MANY OF THEM GUILTY OF SOME OF THE SAME IMPEACHABLE OFFENSES, THEY WILL RESIST IT.

HOWEVER, WE ARE THE AMERICAN PEOPLE AND WE STILL HAVE A RIGHT TO CONTROL OUR GOVERNMENT, AND THE PEOPLE ELECTED TO REPRESENT US. THEREFORE, I AM PERSONALLY CALLING ON THE CONSERVATIVE MEMBERS THE HOUSE OF

REPRESENTATIVES TO BRING THIS ACTION BASED ON THE GROUNDS I HAVE ENUMERATED SO THAT THE AMERICAN PEOPLE CAN UNDERSTAND WHAT IS REALLY AT STAKE HERE. THEN "WE THE PEOPLE," CAN MAKE OUR VOICES HEARD.

ABOUT THE AUTHOR

Walter Randall Bannister is an American author of ficton and religion. His first two books, Islam Is Of The Devil and Christopher Dorner: Victim Of A Corrupt LAPD have sold about 150,000 copies. Walter was born in Atlanta, Georgia on Thanksgiving Day November 24,1960. He was raised in Newport, Rhode Island. He is an ordained minister and Chaplain with a Doctor Of Divinity and he is a certified Spiritual Counselor.